DATE DUE

GAYLORD   PRINTED IN U.S.A.

SUPER
SANDCASTLE
Going Green

WHAT
IN THE
WRLD
IS
GREEN FOOD?

Oona Gaarder-Juntti

Consulting Editor, Diane Craig, M.A./Reading Specialist

ABDO
Publishing Company

Published by ABDO Publishing Company, 8000 West 78th Street, Edina, Minnesota 55439. Copyright © 2011 by Abdo Consulting Group, Inc. International copyrights reserved in all countries. No part of this book may be reproduced in any form without written permission from the publisher. Super SandCastle™ is a trademark and logo of ABDO Publishing Company.

Printed in the United States of America, North Mankato, Minnesota
052010
092010

 PRINTED ON RECYCLED PAPER

Editor: Katherine Hengel
Content Developer: Nancy Tuminelly
Cover and Interior Design and Production: Oona Gaarder-Juntti, Mighty Media
Photo Credits: AbleStock, iStockphoto (Matteo De Stefano, Kim Gunkel, Liza McCorkle), Shutterstock

Library of Congress Cataloging-in-Publication Data

Gaarder-Juntti, Oona, 1979-
  What in the world is green food? / Oona Gaarder-Juntti.
    p. cm. -- (Going green)
  ISBN 978-1-61613-192-0
  1. Food--Environmental aspects--Juvenile literature. I. Title.
  TX355.G33 2011
  641--dc22
                          2010004321

Super SandCastle™ books are created by a team of professional educators, reading specialists, and content developers around five essential components— phonemic awareness, phonics, vocabulary, text comprehension, and fluency— to assist young readers as they develop reading skills and strategies and increase their general knowledge. All books are written, reviewed, and leveled for guided reading, early reading intervention, and Accelerated Reader® programs for use in shared, guided, and independent reading and writing activities to support a balanced approach to literacy instruction.

ABOUT SUPER SANDCASTLE™

Bigger Books for Emerging Readers

Grades K–4

Created for library, classroom, and at-home use, Super SandCastle™ books support and engage young readers as they develop and build literacy skills and will increase their general knowledge about the world around them. Super SandCastle™ books are an extension of SandCastle™, the leading preK–3 imprint for emerging and beginning readers. Super SandCastle™ features a larger trim size for more reading fun.

Let Us Know

Super SandCastle™ would like to hear your stories about reading this book. What was your favorite page? Was there something hard that you needed help with? Share the ups and downs of learning to read. We want to hear from you! Send us an e-mail.

sandcastle@abdopublishing.com

Contact us for a complete list of SandCastle™, Super SandCastle™, and other nonfiction and fiction titles from ABDO Publishing Company.

www.abdopublishing.com • 8000 West 78th Street Edina, MN 55439 • 800-800-1312 • 952-831-1632 fax

Contents

WHAT IN THE WORLD IS BEING GREEN?

Being green means taking care of the earth. Many things on our planet are connected. When one thing changes, it can cause something else to change. That's why the way we treat the earth is so important. Keeping the earth healthy can seem like a big job. You can help by saving energy and **resources** every day.

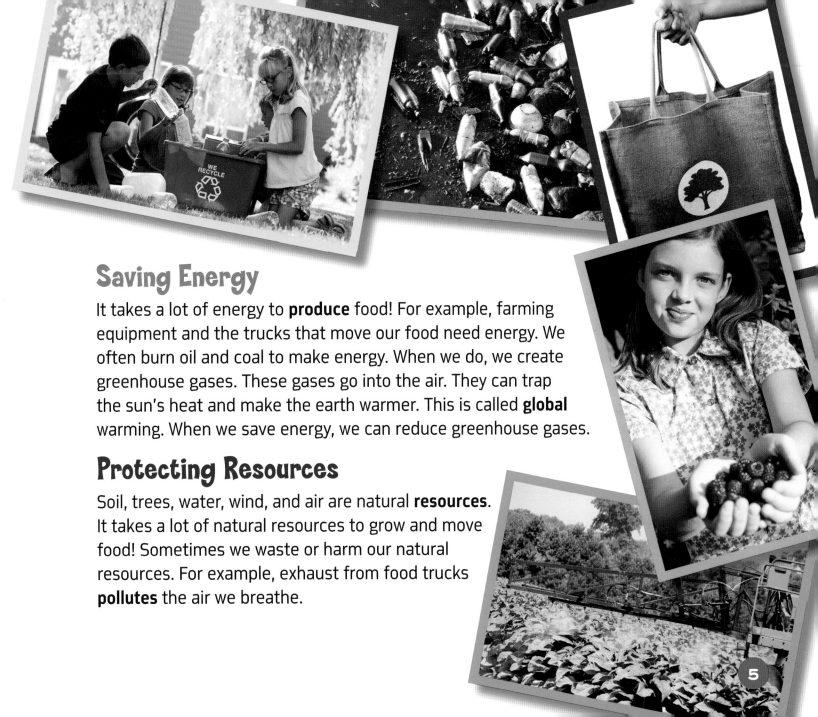

Saving Energy

It takes a lot of energy to **produce** food! For example, farming equipment and the trucks that move our food need energy. We often burn oil and coal to make energy. When we do, we create greenhouse gases. These gases go into the air. They can trap the sun's heat and make the earth warmer. This is called **global** warming. When we save energy, we can reduce greenhouse gases.

Protecting Resources

Soil, trees, water, wind, and air are natural **resources**. It takes a lot of natural resources to grow and move food! Sometimes we waste or harm our natural resources. For example, exhaust from food trucks **pollutes** the air we breathe.

GREEN FOOD

Have you ever thought about where your food comes from? How was it grown or raised? How did it get to your grocery store? Eating green means buying, preparing, and throwing away food in an earth-friendly way. We can make choices that are good for the planet and our bodies!

Did you know?

An average family of four throws away 122 pounds (55 kg) of food every month!

Did you know?

Americans throw away 100 billion plastic bags every year!!

Did you know?

An average meal in the United States has food from five different countries.

Cooking with fresh food tastes better and is better for you.

IN A GREEN WORLD

How food is grown and where it comes from makes a difference. Choosing local foods is one way to help.

Support local farmers by buying food at a farmers market.

★ FARM FRESH ★
LOCALLY GROWN
VEGETABLES
& FRUI

IN A GREEN WORLD

How we treat the earth when we grow food is important! Your choices can make a difference.

Organic farmers rotate their crops. This helps keep the soil healthy.

Organic farmers provide healthy habitats for some birds, insects, and animals. They don't use any chemicals!

You can grow food in your own backyard.

Fruits and vegetables are the freshest right when they are picked.

HOW YOU CAN HELP

Everyone knows the 3 Rs. Reduce, Reuse, and Recycle. Do you know how to practice the 3 Rs with food? The next few pages will show you how! Think about what you eat and where it comes from. There are many simple things we can do to eat green!

Paper or Plastic?

The next time you go shopping, help your family remember to bring reusable bags. It takes energy and **resources** to make plastic and paper bags. Buy a strong, cloth bag instead! Your family can use it over and over again.

Plastic bags can last up to 1,000 years in the **landfill**.

Buy Local

Most food travels more than a 1,000 miles before it gets to you. If you buy local food, it doesn't have to travel so far! This saves energy and **resources**. Local food usually has less packaging too. That means less garbage in **landfills**! Fresh food is very healthy. You can buy local food at farmers markets and co-ops. Some grocery stores put signs by local foods too.

★ FARM FRESH ★
LOCALLY GROWN
VEGETABLES
& FRUITS

Community supported **agriculture** (CSA) programs help you buy food from farmers in your area. Ask your parents if there are CSAs in your area.

Grow Your Own

You can grow your own food! It is easy to grow vegetables in your backyard or in pots. Ask your parents if you can start a family garden. Try tomatoes, lettuce, spinach, green beans, carrots, and radishes. They are easy to grow!

Go Organic

Buy **organic** food when you can. Organic food is grown without harmful chemicals such as **pesticides** or **fertilizers**. That's why organic food is better for you and the land! Organic farmers are very careful with the natural **resources** they use.

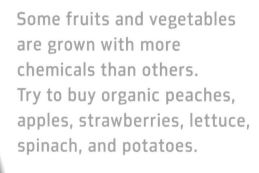

Some fruits and vegetables are grown with more chemicals than others. Try to buy organic peaches, apples, strawberries, lettuce, spinach, and potatoes.

Cook Smart

When you make food, you usually use energy. Microwave ovens, toasters, and stoves all use energy. Try not to waste any! For example, use covers on pots when you can. If you're using the oven, open the door as little as possible. Then the heat doesn't escape! You can share these tips with your family!

Recycle Your Food

Worms love kitchen scraps! Worms are good at reducing food scraps quickly. They eat the scraps and then go to the bathroom. It's a little gross, but it makes great **compost**! This process is called vermicomposting. You can vermicompost at home! Make sure you have the right kind of bin for your worms. Plastic, wood, and Styrofoam containers work well. Metal containers can get too hot for your worms!

Fresh Cooking

Make your own food instead of buying prepared food. When you cook from scratch, you know what goes into your food. Cooking is fun! Help your parents plan homemade meals. You can find recipes in cookbooks and help make dinner!

Try not to waste food. Make only as much food as you'll be able to eat. Or eat the leftovers at the next meal.

LET'S THINK GREEN

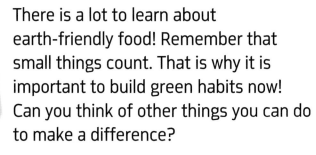

There is a lot to learn about earth-friendly food! Remember that small things count. That is why it is important to build green habits now! Can you think of other things you can do to make a difference?

Taking care of the earth is everyone's responsibility. That means kids and adults! Talk with your family and friends about green foods. Let's all work hard together and think green!

TAKE THE GREEN PLEDGE

I promise to help the earth every day by doing things in a different way.

I can help by:

♻ Bringing my own bag to the store.

♻ Eating food with less packaging.

♻ Saving energy when cooking food.

♻ Buying food from local farmers.

GLOSSARY

agriculture – the science of producing crops and raising animals for sale.

compost – a mixture of natural materials, such as food scraps and lawn clippings, that can turn into fertilizer over time.

fertilizer – something used to make plants grow better in soil.

global – having to do with the whole earth.

landfill – a place where garbage is stacked and then covered up with earth.

organic – using only natural products instead of chemicals.

pesticide – a chemical used to kill pests such as insects.

pollute – to contaminate the air, water, or soil with man-made waste.

produce – to make or grow something.

resource – the supply or source of something. A *natural resource* is a resource found in nature, such as water or trees.